SCIENCE WITH STUFF

DINO-MITE

By Sarah Parvis

downtown bookworks

downtown bookworks

Designed by Georgia Rucker
Typeset in Bryant Pro and Warugaki

Paleontology Consultant: Kierstin Rosenbach

PHOTO CREDITS Front cover: ©iStockPhoto.com/XiaImages (*T. rex*), Jennifer Agster/Shutterstock.com (ground). 1: Herschel Hoffmeyer/Shutterstock.com. 3: Kostyantyn Ivanyshen/Shutterstock.com. 4–5: ©iStockPhoto.com/CoreyFord. 6: ©Mohamad Haghani/Stocktrek Images/Science Source. 7: Herschel Hoffmeyer/Shutterstock.com (*Diplodocus*), Catmando/Shutterstock.com (*Styracosaurus*). 8: ©Gary Hincks/Science Source. 9: ©Ted Kinsman/Science Source (tools), Courtesy of National Park Service (Dinosaur National Park). 10: ©Millard H. Sharp/Science Source (*Triceratops* skin), Herschel Hoffmeyer/Shutterstock.com (*Triceratops*). 11: Rattana/Shutterstock.com (theropod footprint), ©Francois Gohier/ardea.com/P/Pantheon/SuperStock (dinosaur tracks in Chile). 12: Warpaint/Shutterstock.com (all). 13: Warpaint/Shutterstock.com (*Edmontosaurus*), Catmando/Shutterstock.com (*Ceratosaurus*), Linda Bucklin/Shutterstock.com *Centrosaurus*). 14: Catmando/Shutterstock.com (*Brachiosaurus*), ©Stocktrek Images/SuperStock (*Pisanosaurus*). 15: Catmando/Shutterstock.com (*Mamenchisaurus*), David Roland/Shutterstock.com (*Argentinosaurus*), Elenarts/Shutterstock.com (background). 16: Warpaint/Shutterstock.com (*Velociraptor, Protoceratops*), ©Millard H. Sharp/Science Source (*Velociraptor* bones), Sarunyu L/Shutterstock.com (*Protoceratops* bones). 17: ©iStockPhoto.com/mariephoto28 (*Allosaurus*), Faviel_Raven/Shutterstock.com (*Allosaurus* bones), Herschel Hoffmeyer/Shutterstock.com (*Giganotosaurus*), ©DeAgostini/SuperStock (*Eoraptor*). 18: ©Universal Images Group North America LLC/DeAgostini/Alamy Stock Photo (teeth), Oleksiy Maksymenko/imageBROKER/SuperStock (*Pachycephalosaurus*), ©Colin Keates/Dorling Kindersley/Natural History Museum, London/Science Source (spoon-shaped tooth). 19: releon8211/Shutterstock.com (*T. rex*), ©Kim Steele/Exactostock-1598/SuperStock (teeth). 20: ©MasPix/Alamy Stock Photo. 21: Elenarts/Shutterstock.com (*Euoplocephalus*), Herschel Hoffmeyer/Shutterstock.com (*Stegosaurus*), Catmando/Shutterstock.com (*Apatosaurus*). 22–23: Kostyantyn Ivanyshen/Shutterstock.com. 24–25: Michael Rosskothen/Shutterstock.com. 26: David Herraez Calzada/Shutterstock.com (*Triceratops* skull), David Roland/Shutterstock.com (*Triceratops*). 27: Bob Orsillo/Shutterstock.com (*Einiosaurus*), Linda Bucklin/Shutterstock.com (*Styracosaurus*), Valentyna Chukhlyebova/Shutterstock.com (*Protoceratops*), Sofia Santos/Shutterstock.com (*Zuniceratops*), Michael Rosskothen/Shutterstock.com (*Pentaceratops*). 28: ©Warpaint/Shutterstock.com (*Lambeosaurus*), Linda Bucklin/Shutterstock.com (*Corythosaurus*). 29: Michael Rosskothen/Shutterstock.com (*Dilophosaurus*), Catmando/Shutterstock.com (*Parasaurolophus*). 30: Catmando/Shutterstock.com. 31: Michael Rosskothen/Shutterstock.com (*Sauropelta*), Warpaint/Shutterstock.com (*Euoplocephalus*), Herschel Hoffmeyer/Shutterstock.com (*Saltasaurus*). 32: Michael Rosskothen/Shutterstock.com (*Microraptor*), ©Nobumichi Tamura/Stocktrek Images/Science Source (*Psittacosaurus*). 33: ©Alvaro Rozalen/Stocktrek Images/Science Source (*Sinosauropteryx*), Herschel Hoffmeyer (*Velociraptor*). 34–35: Elenarts/Shutterstock.com (*Argentinosaurus*), ©Brian Engh/CC-BY (*Aquilops*), Linda Bucklin/Shutterstock.com (all others). 36–37: ©Stocktrek Images/SuperStock. 37: ©Wolfgang Kaehler/age fotostock/SuperStock. 38: Jaroslav Moravcik/Shutterstock.com (eggs bottom left), ©Millard H. Sharp/Science Source (*Psittacosaurus* egg). 39: Linda Bucklin/Shutterstock.com (*Psittacosaurus*), ©DeAgostini/SuperStock (*Maiasura*). 40: Suchatbky/Shutterstock.com (horseshoe crab), LAURA_VN/Shutterstock.com (crab), Somchai Buddha/Shutterstock.com (shrimp), Aleksandar Dickov/Shutterstock.com (snail), Edward Westmacott/Shutterstock.com (lobster), JIANG HONGYAN/Shutterstock.com (clam), Ratikova/Shutterstock.com (sea star), Evlakhov Valeriy/Shutterstock.com (lamprey). 41: Shu Ba/Shutterstock.com (sea cucumber), fivespots/Shutterstock.com (snake), Honey Cloverz/Shutterstock.com (tuatara), Michiel de Wit/Shutterstock.com (frog), Eric Isselee/Shutterstock.com (echidna), ©iStockPhoto.com/JohnCarnemolla (platypus), wacpan/Shutterstock.com (scorpion), vnlit/Shutterstock.com (dragonfly), irin-k/Shutterstock.com (bee), sumroeng chinnapan/Shutterstock.com (cockroach), ©Christian Jegou/Publiphoto/Science Source (Cretaceous scene). 42: ©Photononstop/SuperStock. 43: Photo by Greg Erickson. 44: ©Francois Gohier/ardea.com/P/Pantheon/SuperStock (*Apatosaurus* bones), ©iStockPhoto.com/emyerson (*Apatosaurus*), Elenarts/Shutterstock.com (*Caudipteryx*). 45: ©DeAgostini/SuperStock (*Mussaurus*), Ozja/Shutterstock.com (*Parasaurolophus*), ©Stocktrek Images/SuperStock (*Oviraptor*). 46: ©iStockPhoto.com/gfrandsen. 47: ©Richard Bizley/Science Source. 48: Warpaint/Shutterstock.com. Back cover: Valentina Chukhlyebova/Shutterstock.com (*Spinosaurus*), Jennifer Agster/Shutterstock.com (ground).

Printed in China, April 2017
ISBN 9781941367421
10 9 8 7 6 5 4 3 2 1

Downtown Bookworks Inc.
265 Canal Street
New York, NY 10013
www.downtownbookworks.com

CONTENTS

WHEN DINOS RULED

Long before the first humans appeared, dinosaurs roamed the Earth. For about 160 million years, these reptiles lived, ate, had babies, fought, and died. Lucky for us, they left behind a lot of fossil evidence so we can make educated guesses about what their lives were like.

All dinosaurs lived during the Mesozoic era. They lived and moved on land, standing upright with their legs beneath them (unlike crocodiles, whose legs jut out to the sides). Flying pterosaurs and swimming ichthyosaurs lived at the same time, but they were not dinosaurs.

THE AGE OF THE DINOSAUR

Dinosaurs lived during the Mesozoic era, from about 250 million years ago to 65 million years ago. The Mesozoic era is broken up into three periods: the Triassic, Jurassic, and Cretaceous periods.

TRIASSIC PERIOD • 250–201 MILLION YEARS AGO

The land was mostly hot and dry. The world's first dinosaurs appeared about 230 million years ago.

Herrerasaurus is one of the earliest known dinosaurs. It walked on two legs and had three long, curved claws on its front feet. At 10 feet long, it was small compared to the dinosaurs that came later!

JURASSIC PERIOD
200–145 MILLION YEARS AGO

The climate changed during this period. Forests, jungles, and big leafy plants took over places that had been dry and desertlike. The first mammals and birds appeared. And many, many dinosaurs roamed the planet.

Giant, plant-eating dinosaurs like the **Diplodocus** thrived in the Jurassic period. Some people call this period the Age of Giants because of the huge dinos!

CRETACEOUS PERIOD
144–65 MILLION YEARS AGO

Flowering plants began to grow. The continents moved apart. And horned dinosaurs appeared. By the late Cretaceous period, there were more types of dinosaurs than ever before.

Styracosaurus was one of the large, horned dinosaurs that roamed North America in the Cretaceous period.

BURIED TREASURES

It took millions of years for the bones, teeth, and poop of dinosaurs to turn into fossils. The conditions had to be just right.

Many dinosaur fossils come from dinosaurs that died in or near water. Their bodies sank into the mud. Layers of mud, sand, or gravel covered them. Slowly, the mud and the body were buried deeper in the earth. Eventually, the mud turned into rock. Minerals from the earth seeped into the dinosaur remains. These minerals changed the bones into fossils.

How were the fossils uncovered? Sometimes scientists or explorers went digging to find them. Other times, nature and weather uncovered them. Wind, rain, and ice carried away bits of earth. Over millions of years, they even wore down mountains! Sometimes, buried remains ended up back on the surface again.

Paleontologists use hammers, chisels, paintbrushes, and other tools to carefully uncover dinosaur bones.

Dinosaur National Park is in Utah and Colorado. Visitors can see lots of dinosaur bones sticking out of the ground.

FOSSILS TELL TALES

Triceratops skin

Not all parts of dinosaurs turned into fossils. Most were broken into tiny bits by other animals or bacteria. Wind, water, and weather also broke down dinosaur remains. It is a lucky day when someone finds a dinosaur fossil!

Triceratops

The most common dinosaur fossils are bones and teeth. Finding softer body parts, like muscles and skin, is rare.

As dinosaurs marched across the land, they sometimes left footprints in the mud. Over time, this mud turned to rock. These imprint fossils are clues! Scientists can act like detectives and study ancient footprints for information about a dinosaur's size and weight. Did the dinosaur drag its tail? Did it have claws? Footprints can help us see where dinosaurs went. And they can tell us how fast a dinosaur was moving, too!

100 million-year-old theropod footprint in Thailand

A large dinosaur's back feet could be 3 feet wide! How big are your feet?

These dinosaur tracks in Chile are about 145 million years old.

There is a name for studying dino tracks. It is paleoichnology!

PREHISTORIC GROUPS

Dinosaurs are divided into groups based on the shape of their hip bones, what they ate, how they moved, and how they behaved. Here are some common groups.

Dinosaur names can be tricky! The names of some dinosaurs are just like the names of the group they belong to. The word "hadrosaur" refers to a type of dinosaur. And *Hadrosaurus* is one particular dinosaur in that group. *Ankylosaurus* is just one type of ankylosaur. Get it?

Shunosaurus

Polacanthus

SAUROPODS
These huge herbivores walked on four legs. They had long necks and long legs. *Examples: Brachiosaurus, Camarasaurus, Shunosaurus*

ANKYLOSAURS
Ankylosaurs are armored dinosaurs. These heavy, four-legged dinos are herbivores. *Examples: Ankylosaurus, Hylaeosaurus, Polacanthus*

HADROSAURS

Hadrosaurs were the duck-billed dinosaurs. These herbivores had flat snouts. Their beaks were toothless, but they had lots and lots of teeth along their cheeks.
Examples: Edmontosaurus, Lambeosaurus, Maiasaura

Edmontosaurus

THEROPODS

All meat-eating dinosaurs belong to this group. Some plant eaters do, too. But most theropods were carnivores that walked on two feet. They had powerful legs and short arms.
Examples: Ceratosaurus, Spinosaurus, Tyrannosaurus rex

Ceratosaurus

CERATOPSIANS

Some early ceratopsians, like *Psittacosaurus*, walked on two legs. But most ceratopsians walked on four legs and had frills around their necks. *Examples: Centrosaurus, Protoceratops, Triceratops*

Centrosaurus

13

PLANT EATERS

There were more plant-eating dinosaurs than meat-eating dinosaurs. Plant eaters are known as **herbivores.** Herbivores ate plants, like ferns, pine trees and pinecones, ginkgo trees, and horsetails. They also ate cycads, which were tall evergreen plants. Sauropods were the biggest plant eaters. They had small heads, heavy bodies, long tails, and extra-long necks.

If a *Brachiosaurus* were alive today, it could stand on the ground and eat food off the top of a four-story building.

Pisanosaurus was one of the earliest-known plant eaters. It was only about 3 feet long.

14

The earliest sauropods walked on their hind legs. But as they grew bigger and bigger over time, they walked on four legs.

Sauropods swallowed plants without chewing. Many swallowed stones. The stones may have helped grind up the plants in the dinosaurs' stomach. Other, smaller plant eaters ate the ferns and mosses closer to the ground.

Many plant-eating dinosaurs, like the *Mamenchisaurus*, traveled in groups for safety.

Argentinosaurus was enormous. It could grow to be 120 feet long.

MEAT EATERS

T. rex is the most famous meat-eating dinosaur, but it is not the only one. Some meat eaters, or **carnivores**, were small. Small carnivores ate insects, lizards, small mammals, and eggs. *Saltopus* weighed only about 5 pounds. It ate insects. *Velociraptors* were also small—about the size of a turkey or a big dog. But they were fierce! They ate small mammals, insects, and small reptiles. They even ate other tiny dinosaurs.

Velociraptors had a long, sharp claw on each back foot. They used this bladelike claw to slash prey.

A *T. rex* could eat 500 pounds in one bite.

The **Protoceratops** used its beak as a powerful weapon.

Large meat eaters, like *Allosaurus* and *T. rex*, had powerful jaws and teeth like knives. They went after bigger meals, like other dinosaurs.

Some predators hunted alone. Others, like the small quick *Coelophysis*, hunted in packs. *Suchomimus* ate lots of fish.

Allosaurus grew to be 30 to 40 feet long. At the end of its short, strong arms, it had three hooked claws.

One of the earliest meat eaters was **Eoraptor.** This 3-foot-long dino had light hollow bones, like birds do today.

Giganotosaurus was probably the biggest meat eater. It was about 46 feet long.

17

TERRIFYING TEETH

Dinosaur teeth came in many shapes and sizes.

Hadrosaurs had more teeth than any other dinosaur—up to 1,400!

A dinosaur's teeth can tell you what it ate. Meat-eating dinosaurs used their teeth to kill their prey. Their teeth were strong and sharp like knives. They could slice through thick reptile skin and even crunch through bone.

But meat eaters were not the only ones with strong teeth! Pine needles and pinecones are hard to chew. Hadrosaurs needed strong teeth to grind up tough plant parts.

Apatosaurus had teeth but did not use them to chew. Instead, it used them to strip leaves off branches. Some dinosaurs, like *Gallimimus* and *Ornithomimus*, didn't have teeth at all.

Many plant eaters, like *Pachycephalosaurus*, *Stegosaurus*, and *Ankylosaurus*, had leaf-shaped or spoon-shaped teeth.

A **T. rex's** teeth were big and thick like bananas. But they had jagged, sawlike edges.

TERRIFIC TAILS

Dinosaur tails were not just for show. They helped dinosaurs get around and stay safe. *T. rex*, *Allosaurus*, and other dinos walked on two legs. Most of their body weight was up front. Their heavy tails kept them from falling forward. While running, they could flick their tail one way or the other to turn quickly. A quick turn could help a dinosaur chase down prey or escape a predator! Some huge herbivores leaned back on their tails to reach high up into the trees.

Diplodocus's tail was made up of about 80 bones and could be up to 43 feet long! That is longer than most school buses!

Ankylosauruses could swing their heavy tails when they were attacked by a predator like *T. rex*.

Ankylosaurs, like *Euoplocephalus*, had a club at the end of their tail. They could swing it and knock over a predator— or even break its leg. These clubs could be more than 3 feet wide!

Stegosaurus had spikes on its tail. The group of spikes at the end of its tail is called a "thagomizer."

Sauropods, like *Apatosaurus*, *Barosaurus*, and *Diplodocus*, may have used their long, thin tails as whips!

21

SAIL-BACKED DINOS

Spinosaurus

Spinosaurus fossils were first found in Egypt.

Spinosaurus lived mostly in the water. It had a snout like a crocodile's and paddlelike feet.

The flat thing sticking up from a *Spinosaurus*'s back is called a sail. It is made up of long bones and covered with skin. Veins beneath the skin carry warm blood throughout the dinosaur's body. Many scientists believe that the large surface of the sail allowed heat to escape from the animal, keeping it cool on a hot day. Sails may also have been used to attract mates or to store extra body fat.

Sails may have kept some animals safer. They made dinosaurs look much bigger and harder to beat in a fight. Also, if a predator chomped down on a dinosaur's sail, it would not hit any major organs. The injured animal could still get away and live.

23

WHAT WERE THE PLATES FOR?

Like the sail on the back of *Spinosaurus*, the plates on the back of *Stegosaurus* may have helped the dinosaur stay warm or cool down. Perhaps *Stegosaurus* showed off its plates to say "hello" to other members of the same species or to find a mate.

The plates were probably also used for protection. Slow-moving plant eaters needed all the help they could get to stay safe from fast-moving, meat-eating predators. The plates made a *Stegosaurus* look much bigger. A predator might not want to take on such a large animal.

Plus, how could an attacking dinosaur jump on a *Stegosaurus*'s back with all those bony plates there? Ouch!

Each spike on a *Stegosaurus's* deadly tail could be up to 4 feet long!

Stegosaurus had two rows of tall plates. They went from its neck to its tail.

The plates are called "scutes." They were bony but not completely solid.

Stegosaurus had a beak. Scientists have found teeth that were not worn down. They think the stegosaurs may have just swallowed ferns whole.

Stegosaurus had one of the smallest brains of all the dinosaurs. One scientist described its brain as the size and shape of a bent hot dog!

25

HORNS AND FRILLS

Triceratops looks tough. And it certainly was. But it did not use its horns for hunting. It was not even a meat eater. Many scientists think the horns were mostly for display. An extra-large horn might attract a mate or frighten other *Triceratops*.

When a *Triceratops* was young, its horns were short and stubby. They curved backward. The horns straightened out as the dino grew up. Later, the horns pointed forward.

Triceratops had a short nose horn and two giant horns that were about 3¼ feet long. That's probably just a little bit shorter than you!

The bony ruffle around *Triceratops*'s head is called a **frill.** It was made of solid bone. The frills of different dinosaurs had different shapes. Some had spikes, horns, or bumps on them.

Einiosaurus had two horns on its frill. It also had a big, curved horn above its nose.

Styracosaurus had a big nose horn and a frill with six spikes on the end.

Zuniceratops was only 10 to 11 feet long. It had brow horns but no nose horn.

Protoceratops was only as big as a sheep. It had a frill but no horns.

Pentaceratops had a head frill, three horns, and two spikes beneath its eyes.

CRESTS UP TOP!

Lambeosaurus, *Parasaurolophus*, and *Corythosaurus* were hadrosaurs with funky shapes on the tops of their heads. These growths are called **crests**.

Scientists think these dinosaurs may have made noises by blowing air through their crest. Different shapes would have made different noises.

Some scientists think dinosaur crests had colorful patterns.

Lambeosaurus's tall crest pointed forward.

Corythosaurus's crest looked like a fin on top of its head.

Some meat-eating dinosaurs also had crests. The 20-foot-long *Dilophosaurus* is one of them. It had a double crest on its head. Not all *Dilophosauruses* had crests. Some experts think only the males had them.

The first *Dilophosaurus* skeleton was found In Arizona in the 1940s.

Dilophosaurus

Parasaurolophus's hollow crest could be 6 feet long.

SKIN LIKE ARMOR

What is huge and strong and spiky all over? An *Ankylosaurus*! And it is not the only dinosaur to have super-tough armor-plated skin. *Edmontonia*, *Panoplosaurus*, and *Sauropelta* are other armored dinosaurs in the ankylosaur group.

Even an ankylosaur's eyelids were covered in armor!

Ankylosaurus was built like a tank! It was low to the ground and very heavy.

The bony knobs or plates on the dinosaur's skin were called **osteoderms.** Osteoderms covered most of these dinosaurs' body. Often only the belly was left without armor.

Sauropelta had incredible spikes on its shoulders and bony knobs all over.

Euoplocephalus had osteoderms on its back and face.

Saltasaurus is an example of a giant sauropod with armored skin. This dinosaur was not named after the salt you put on food. The first *Saltasaurus* fossils were found near Salta, Argentina.

31

WHAT DID DINOS LOOK LIKE?

Microraptors were about the size of crows. They had long, shimmering feathers.

Most scientists now agree: Some dinosaurs had feathers. The feathers were not the right shape for flying. Fluffy feathers may have kept the giant reptiles warm. They were probably also for show. Think of a peacock's big, beautiful tail feathers or the pointy crest on top of a cardinal's head. Bright feathers and shimmery feathers can be used to show off or attract a mate.

Psittacosaurus had bristles or quills on its tail.

Scientists are not sure what dinosaur skin looked like. Some dinosaurs may have had thick leathery skin like an elephant has. Perhaps others had green, scaly skin, like an iguana has. Green skin may have allowed them to hide among ferns and plant leaves. Desert dinosaurs may have been sandy colored to blend into their surroundings. They may even have had stripes or spots like a leopard, tiger, or zebra.

Scientists think *Sinosauropteryx* had orange feathers and a striped tail.

Fossils show that *Velociraptors* had feathers.

Some feathered dinosaurs evolved into birds. That's right—the sparrow in your yard is a descendant of a dinosaur!

DINOSAURS, BIG AND SMALL

Some dinosaurs, like the enormous *Argentinosaurus*, grew to be 120 feet long. At nearly 100 tons, the *Argentinosaurus* is heavier than 15 African elephants!

Argentinosaurus ate a lot. It did not chew its food. It tore tons of leaves off the trees and swallowed them whole.

Argentinosaurus

Camarasaurus   *Giganotosaurus*

Others, like the small, feathered *Microraptor*, weighed only 2 to 5 pounds. A huge titanosaur, like *Argentinosaurus*, kept its feet on the ground. The *Microraptor* probably spent its time in the trees.

Aquilops is a newly discovered dinosaur. It was only as big as a bunny!

Some scientists think the *Torosaurus* is actually a really big *Triceratops*. They will keep studying to find out.

Compsognathus was about the size of a chicken. This fierce, fast little dinosaur was a skilled hunter. It had sharp teeth and good eyesight.

Torosaurus   Dilophosaurus   Ornitholestes   Compsognathus

TOO FAST, TOO SLOW

Panoplosaurus

Ornithomimus

Some dinosaurs sped across the ground on two legs. Others stood firmly on four hefty legs.

The fastest dinosaurs had long legs and ran on two feet, like an ostrich. *Gallimimus* and *Ornithomimus* were two of these quick-moving dinos. Scientists think they could run as fast as 43 miles per hour. Ask your parents to tell you the next time they are driving 43 miles per hour in the car.

The slowest dinosaurs were huge herbivores like *Mamenchisaurus* and *Apatosaurus*. They had four thick, heavy legs. They were so big that they did not need to run away from predators. Heavy armor-plated dinosaurs like *Panoplosaurus* and *Stegosaurus* were pretty slow, too.

Most two-legged dinosaurs walked on their toes. They moved faster than their four-legged relatives.

Ornithomimus fossil

37

LITTLE EGGS, BIG DINOS

Many dinosaurs buried their eggs. Others, like *Maiasaura*, laid them in nests. They sat on their eggs to keep them warm and safe, just like birds do today.

Before an animal is born or hatched, it is called an embryo. Finding an egg with all of the tiny bones of a dinosaur embryo inside is rare. But some lucky scientists have found them and studied them.

Psittacosaurus eggs were only 3 to 5 inches long. Look at the tiny bones inside!

An adult **Psittacosaurus** could grow to be 6½ feet long.

A *Psittacosaurus* walked on two legs and had a powerful beak, like a parrot.

These eggs give us clues about how dino parents took care of their young. For example, some dinosaurs' bones weren't very hard when they were born. That means the baby dinosaurs could not walk right away. Parent dinosaurs had to feed and care for the babies until they were stronger.

A **Maiasaura** nest

WHAT LIVED WITH DINOSAURS?

Humans and dinosaurs did not live at the same time. Modern humans are called *Homo sapiens*. And we did not exist until about 200,000 years ago. You may see humans running from dinosaurs in the movies, but that never really happened. Those stories are science fiction.

So, who shared the hot, tropical planet with dinosaurs? Dinosaurs ruled the land, but there were other reptiles on the scene. Mostly, they were giant crocodile-like beasts. The mammals of the time were small, like today's shrews or rats.

Many animals alive today lived with the dinosaurs. Most looked a little different back then. But some, like horseshoe crabs, have not changed much at all.

HERE ARE SOME ANIMALS THAT SHARED THE PLANET WITH DINOSAURS.

crabs

shrimp

snails

lobsters

clams

sea stars

lampreys

sea cucumbers

snakes

tuataras

frogs

echidnas

platypuses

scorpions

dragonflies

bees

cockroaches

During the Cretaceous period, birds and pterosaurs soared through the air. Enormous reptiles like ichthyosaurs, mosasaurs, and plesiosaurs swam in the oceans.

41

FOSSIL HUNTERS

Bones of a 135 million-year-old *Jobaria* were found in the Sahara desert, in Niger. It was as hot as 120°F when scientists pulled tons of rock and bone from the ground.

There are dinosaur fossils on every continent. These fossils might be right under our feet. They may be trapped under many layers of dirt, sand, mud, snow, ice, and asphalt. Or they may be hidden beneath the ocean floor.

A paleontologist is a scientist who examines fossils and studies the history of life on Earth. Paleontologists may need to go to remote places, hike for long distances, dig deep into the earth, explore dark caves, or climb rock faces to find fossils.

Scientists recently uncovered dinosaur bones in northern Alaska. They had to work on cold, snowy days. They took inflatable rafts and used ropes to climb down cliffs to get to the bones. Alaska was warmer back when the *Ugrunaaluk* dino was alive!

OOOOPS!

What we know about dinosaurs changes as scientists find more fossils and learn new things. Here are a few ideas about dinosaurs that have changed over the years.

WE'RE THE SAME!

For many years, every dinosaur fan knew all about the huge, long-necked *Brontosaurus*. Then scientists figured out that the *Brontosaurus* was the same animal as the *Apatosaurus*.

Scientists used to think all dinosaurs had dull, gray leathery skin. But now, they know that some dinos, like *Caudipteryx*, had feathers.

LOOK! FEATHERS!

44

Paleontologists once found the tiny bones of a dinosaur and named it *Mussaurus*. That means "mouse lizard." Later, they discovered that the bones belonged to a baby dino, not a tiny dino. An adult mouse lizard could weigh 250 pounds!

WAY BIGGER THAN A MOUSE!

Some scientists thought *Parasaurolophus* spent time in the water. They even thought it could breathe through its crest. Now we know that is not true.

AS IF!

I'M NO THIEF!

A fossil hunter found bones around a bunch of eggs and named the dinosaur *Oviraptor*. That means "egg thief." Later, paleontologists figured out that the dinosaur was sitting on its own eggs. It was protecting them, not stealing them!

45

WHAT IS A COPROLITE?

The fossil that comes with this book was once dinosaur poop. Now it is a coprolite. Coprolites are like other fossils. Over millions of years, the poop absorbed minerals and turned into a fossil. But don't worry! The coprolite does not smell, and it is clean and safe to touch. Hold the fossil in your hand and think: "Wow! Millions of years ago, this was dino poop!"

The coprolite that comes with this book has been cleaned and polished.

Scientists can study coprolites to find out what dinosaurs ate. They might find seeds, parts of leaves, fish scales, or wood in the coprolites. Are there bits of bone in a coprolite? That can show whether a dinosaur was a carnivore or an herbivore.

Early dinosaurs lived surrounded by ferns, horsetails, and moss. Scientists thought grass did not appear until after the dinosaurs died out. But then they found grass in some dinosaur coprolites. Now we know that grass began to grow on Earth before dinosaurs went extinct. See! Scientists can learn a lot from poop.

HOW DO I SAY THAT? Saying dinosaur names can be hard. This guide can help.

Allosaurus	AL-oh-SOR-us	Microraptor	MY-croh-RAP-tor
Ankylosaurus	ang-KAI-lo-SOR-us	Morelladon	moh-RAY-oh-don
Apatosaurus	ah-PAT-oh-SOR-us	Mussaurus	moo-SOR-us
Aquilops	ah-QUILL-ops	Ornitholestes	or-nith-oh-LESS-teez
Argentinosaurus	ar-jen-TEEN-oh-SOR-us	Ornithomimus	or-NITH-oh-MIME-us
Barosaurus	BARE-uh-SOR-us	Ouranosaurus	YOO-ray-noh-SOR-us
Brachiosaurus	BRAK-ee-oh-SOR-us	Oviraptor	OH-vee-RAP-tor
Camarasaurus	KAM-er-ah-SOR-us	Pachycephalosaurus	PAK-ee-SEFF-uh-loh-SOR-us
Caudipteryx	cow-DIP-tuh-riks	Panoplosaurus	pan-OH-plo-SOR-us
Centrosaurus	SEN-tro-SOR-us	Parasaurolophus	PAIR-oh-SOR-oh-LO-fuss
Ceratosaurus	suh-RAT-oh-SOR-us	Pentaceratops	PEN-tuh-SAIR-uh-tops
Coelophysis	SEE-lo-FY-sis	Pisanosaurus	pee-SAH-noh-SOR-us
Compsognathus	comp-sog-NAY-thus	Polacanthus	pol-uh-KAN-thus
Corythosaurus	ko-RITH-oh-SORE-us	Protoceratops	PROH-toh-SAIR-uh-tops
Dilophosaurus	die-LOAF-oh-SOR-us	Psittacosaurus	SIT-uh-koh-SOR-us
Diplodocus	dih-PLOD-uh-kuss	Saltasaurus	SALT-uh-SOR-us
Edmontonia	ed-mon-TOH-nee-uh	Saltopus	SALT-oh-puss
Edmontosaurus	ed-MON-toh-SOR-us	Sauropelta	SORE-oh-PEL-tuh
Einiosaurus	EYE-nee-oh-SOR-us	Shunosaurus	SHOON-oh-SOR-us
Eoraptor	EE-oh-RAP-tor	Sinosauropteryx	SINE-oh-saw-ROP-tuh-riks
Euoplocephalus	YOO-oh-plo-SEFF-uh-luss	Spinosaurus	SPINE-oh-SOR-us
Gallimimus	GAL-ih-MIME-us	Stegosaurus	STEG-oh-SOR-us
Giganotosaurus	JIG-an-OH-toh-SOR-us	Styracosaurus	sty-RAK-oh-SOR-us
Hadrosaurus	HAD-ro-SOR-us	Suchomimus	SOOK-oh-MIME-us
Herrerasaurus	huh-RARE-uh-SOR-us	Torosaurus	TOR-oh-SOR-us
Hylaeosaurus	hi-LEE-oh-SOR-us	Triceratops	tri-SAIR-uh-tops
Jobaria	joh-BAH-ree-uh	Tyrannosaurus rex	tih-RAN-oh-SOR-us REKS
Lambeosaurus	LAM-bee-oh-SOR-us	Ugrunaaluk	oo-GREW-nah-luk
Maiasaura	MY-ah-SORE-uh	Velociraptor	vell-OSS-ih-RAP-tor
Mamenchisaurus	ma-MEN-chee-SOR-us	Zuniceratops	ZOO-nee-SAIR-uh-tops

WANT TO LEARN MORE ABOUT DINOSAURS? READ ON!

Curious About Fossils by Kate Waters (Grosset & Dunlap, 2016).

Dining with Dinosaurs: A Tasty Guide to Mesozoic Munching by Hannah Bonner (National Geographic Kids, 2016).

Everything You Need to Know About Dinosaurs and Other Prehistoric Creatures by John Woodward (DK, 2014).

How to Draw Ferocious Dinosaurs and Other Prehistoric Creatures by Fiona Gowen (Barron's Educational Series, 2016).

Jurassic Poop: What Dinosaurs (and Others) Left Behind by Jacob Berkowitz, illustrated by Steve Mack (Kids Can Press, 2006).

National Geographic Little Kids First Big Book of Dinosaurs by Catherine D. Hughes, illustrated by Franco Tempesta (National Geographic Kids, 2011).

Prehistoric Predators by Brian Switek, illustrated by Julius Csotonyi (Applesauce Press, 2015).

The Big Book of Dinosaurs by Angela Wilkes and Darren Naish (DK, 2015).

Ultimate Dinosaurs by Douglas Palmer (DK, 2013).

Why Did T. rex Have Short Arms? And Other Questions About... Dinosaurs by Melissa Stewart (Sterling Children's Books, 2014).